YOUR KNOWLEDGE HAS VALUE

Anne-Kathrin Busè

Euthanasia - An overview about forms, differences and difficulties

GRIN Verlag

Bibliografische Information der Deutschen Nationalbibliothek:

Die Deutsche Bibliothek verzeichnet diese Publikation in der Deutschen National-
bibliografie; detaillierte bibliografische Daten sind im Internet über http://dnb.d-
nb.de/ abrufbar.

Imprint:

Copyright © 2006 GRIN Verlag GmbH
Druck und Bindung: Books on Demand GmbH, Norderstedt Germany
ISBN: 978-3-640-20546-2

This book at GRIN:

http://www.grin.com/en/e-book/117387/euthanasia-an-overview-about-forms-dif-
ferences-and-difficulties

GRIN - Your knowledge has value

Der GRIN Verlag publiziert seit 1998 wissenschaftliche Arbeiten von Studenten, Hochschullehrern und anderen Akademikern als eBook und gedrucktes Buch. Die Verlagswebsite www.grin.com ist die ideale Plattform zur Veröffentlichung von Hausarbeiten, Abschlussarbeiten, wissenschaftlichen Aufsätzen, Dissertationen und Fachbüchern.

Visit us on the internet:

http://www.grin.com/

http://www.facebook.com/grincom

http://www.twitter.com/grin_com

Euthanasia –
An overview about forms, differences and difficulties

0.	**„Hook" of the presentation**	**1**
1.	**Introduction**	**1**
2.	**Forms of euthanasia**	**1**
	a) Passive euthanasia	1
	b) Active (or direct) euthanasia	2
	c) Active homicide	2
	d) Indirect euthanasia	2
	e) Assisted suicide	2
3.	**The situation within Germany and the relevant laws**	**3**
4.	**Situation in other european countries**	**4**
	a) The Netherlands and Belgium	4
	b) Switzerland	5
	c) Other european countries	5
5.	**Possible alternatives to euthanasia**	**5**
6.	**Difficulties of euthanasia**	**6**
7.	**Arguments in favour of and against euthanasia**	**7**
8.	**Conclusion**	**8**
9.	**Literatur**	**9**
	Appendix: Well-known cases of euthanasia	**9**

0. „Hook" of the presentation

Imagine the situation: If somebody you love is in serious and ongoing pain and they asked you to help them to die. What would you do?...

1. Introduction

Because of the great advances in medicine and the ever increasing average age in Europe, a discussion of the topic of euthanasia has come to the fore in the last years. The term „euthanasia" originally comes from Greek and means „good death". In ancient Greek society it meant the right of the individual to choose his own form of death, for example if he no longer felt, that living his life had any value. „Good death", or euthanasia, involved a process of fast and easy death, without great suffering. However within Christian belief suicide is regarded as a sin, and therefore, the original meaning of euthanasia has been greatly altered. Today it means medical professionals helping incurably ill people, in order to spare them from agonizing suffering. Another negative connotation of „euthanasia" is its use in genocide during the second world war, when certain people, who were considered inferior such as jews, handicapped people, seriously ill people etc. were exterminated. The Nazis claimed, this was for the benefit of the suffering person and for the benefit of the general public. This is one of the reasons why a discussion about the topic has been such a taboo in Germany for many years, so that an objective and critical examination of this issue is long overdue.

In such a complex discussion there can be no easy solutions, and inevitably there will always be strong and differing opinions. Perhaps the best solution lies in a compromise being found by all sides, and by people informing themselves about the facts and circumstances of euthanasia. The aim of my presentation is to provide some information on the subject, and I would hope to make the recipients think about the issue and to encourage them to discuss it afterwards.

2. Forms of euthanasia

We have to distinguish between active and passive euthanasia, which cannot always clearly be differentiated from each other.

a) Passive euthanasia...

...means to „let die". An example is, when a doctor refuses to give or stops the treatment of life-preserving measures, for instance artificial respiration, dialysis, reanimation or total parenteral nutrition. In this case, the doctor doesn't intervene actively in the medical treatment. For a long time this form has been recognized as a practice in the end stages of an incurable illness. If the doctor helps a patient who is dying, so long as the dying process has already started, the doctor remains unpunished. This form of euthanasia is only punishable by law, if it was practiced without the agreement of the patient and/or if there was no evidence that the patient was already nearing death. Passive euthanasia is only permissible, if medical treatment, for example life-preserving measures, would diminish the right of a person to die with dignity.

b) Active (or direct) euthanasia...

...means homicide on demand by the patient through intervention from the outside, mostly through a doctor. This form of euthanasia is not allowed to be practiced in Germany, even if the patient demands it explicitly. The medical procedure would be to administer poisonous substances, ot to give an overdose of medicine or anaesthetics.

c) Active homicide

For this form of euthanasia the doctor decides autonomously to kill a patient without any agreement from the patient concerned - for instance a person in coma vigil. The doctor and his nursing staff nonetheless get punished for commiting a homicide, without any consideration of their motives. These motives are unimportant for their sentencing.

d) Indirect euthanasia

This form is also seen als a kind of active euthanasia. The doctor gives a patient medicine, for instance a pain-reliever like morphine, knowing, that as a side effect, the treatment will result in the earlier death of the patien. The doctor choses the benefit of easing the patients pain over the longevity of the patient. Indirect euthanasia is allowed in Germany and even required treatment: That is, it would be seen as being against the medical code, if a doctor refused to administer the necessary strong pain-relievers, because he didn't want to be the cause of bringing on the earlier death of the patient. Due to the neglect of the patient's pain, the doctor would probably be punished for failure to render assistance, or even fined for assault.

e) Assisted suicide

A doctor can provide a patient, who has already expressed the wish to die, with all the medical requirements, he needs for suicide, without the danger of being punished himself. But the patient has to take the last step of the process alone. The doctor provides the lethal medicine, but the patient has to take it by himself. Suicide attempts cannot be prosecuted in Germany, and therefore, assisted suicide is also not punishable by law. After handing over the lethal medicine to the patient, the doctor has to leave the room, in order not to be legally liable, because of failure to render assistance. However this is often criticized, because being left alone to die, is not seen as humane practice.

3. The situation within Germany and the relevant laws

No legal regulation about euthanasia exists in Germany, this means that there is no separate law, regarding euthanasia, in the penal code. Therefore, cases of euthanasia can only be dealt with through the existing laws for murder, manslaughter, death on demand and failure to render assistance.

German penal code (excerpt):

---

§ 211 (Mord)

1. Der Mörder wird mit lebenslanger Freiheitsstrafe bestraft.
2. Mörder ist, wer aus Mordlust, zur Befriedigung des Geschlechtstriebs, aus Habgier oder sonst aus niedrigen Beweggründen, heimtückisch oder grausam oder mit gemeingefährlichen Mitteln oder um eine andere Straftat zu ermöglichen oder zu verdecken, einen Menschen tötet.

§ 212 (Totschlag)

1. Wer einen Menschen tötet, ohne Mörder zu sein, wird als Totschläger mit Freiheitsstrafe nicht unter fünf Jahren bestraft.
2. In besonders schweren Fällen ist auf lebenslange Freiheitsstrafe zu erkennen.

§ 216 (Tötung auf Verlangen)

1. Ist jemand durch das ausdrückliche und ernstliche Verlangen des Getöteten zur Tötung bestimmt worden, so ist auf Freiheitsstrafe von sechs Monaten bis zu fünf Jahren zu erkennen.
2. Der Versuch ist strafbar.

> **§ 323c (Unterlassene Hilfeleistung)**
>
> 1. Wer bei Unglücksfällen oder gemeiner Gefahr oder Not nicht Hilfe leistet, obwohl dies
> erforderlich und ihm den Umständen nach zuzumuten, insbesondere ohne erhebliche
> eigene Gefahr und ohne Verletzung anderer wichtiger Pflichten möglich ist, wird mit
> Freiheitsstrafe bis zu einem Jahr oder mit Geldstrafe bestraft.

However the German parliament is working on a legal regulation of the „Patientenverfügung[1]", which means a written order to stop life-preserving measures. We already have the practice, where a patient can write a „Patientenverfügung", but the exact regulations are not yet clear. The ethics commission, set up by the „Bundestag", suggested that a written determined instruction is always needed, so that a medical treatment can only be refused, if the patient is already diagnosed as terminally ill. In addition, these guidelines should always be updated in connection with the changing health situation of the patient, taking into account, the possibility, that he has perhaps changed his mind. The question, as to whether anybody other than the patient can truely assess the patient's situation, and also the question of having the necessary respect for human life in such situations, both, on the part of the doctor and of the patient, remain particularly difficult to answer. The parliament tries to find solutions, which do justice, on the one hand, to fulfilling peoples request to have a dignified death, and on the other, to meeting the understandable demand of doctors for a binding action-scheme, which would offer them security in their medical practice and protect them against judicial consequences. Another important problem is, that for various reasons, it is often not possible to determine, when the exact state of health, previously described by the patient, in which he would no longer want any life-preserving measures, is reached.

4. Situation in other european countries

Ther is an increasing demand for forms of euthanasia in almost every industrial country. The differing practices and laws, withing these countries, lead to much debate. Active euthanasia is only legal today in two european countries. Which ar the Netherlands and Belgium.

a) The Netherlands and Belgium

Dutch and Belgian doctors are allowed, to administer lethal injections, but only within strict criteria, and under supervision of a control commission. The criteria catalogue comprises the following rules: The patient concerned has to have asked for euthanasia, free from outside

---

[1] ...means „order to stop life-preserving measures"

influence, and in a state of clear consciousness. His suffering should already be at a severe level and without the possibility of further medical treatment to relieve it. Before the act of euthanasia can be carried out, the doctor in question must have consulted a colleague, and finally, he has to send a post-euthanasia report to the relevant legal authority. In the Netherlands, there were 2054 cases of euthanasia in 2001 and 1815 cases in 2003. The reduction in cases is mostly due to the fact, that since 2002 the government annually allocates 10 million euros for hospice[2] and palliative[3] medicine.

b) Switzerland

Assisted Suicide is the only form of euthanasia allowed in Switzerland. Swiss doctors, in certain cases, are permitted, to provide a lethal dose of a medicine, to terminally ill patients. However these patients must take the medicine themselves.

c) Other european countries

Within France, Denmark, Sweden, Norway, Slovenia or Hungary is only a conditional and limited practice of passive euthanasia, what is, stopping life-preserving measures.

5. Possible alternatives to euthanasia

Many patients, who ask for euthanasia, often don't have an actual wish to die, but they do want to be able to overcome an often unbearable situation. The decision to chose euthanasia can have various causes, for instance:

  a. The fear of being left alone while dying.
  b. The fear of over-provision of medical care.
  c. The fear of being left dependent on medical maschines
  d. etc.

Patients may demand active euthanasia, because they fear being helpless and suffering great physical pain at the end of their lives. They fear, they wouldn't be able, to bear the pain, and especially not to be able, to bear it alone. However in many cases, effective medical help is a good pain relief therapy. Therefore, the field of pain research should be improved, and this is an area, that has been strongly neglected until now.

---

[2] ...means „care at the end of a person's life"
[3] ...means „ reducing pain/treatment that reduces pain"

Patients' fears should always be taken seriously, but patients must also be fully informed of the other options, available to them, for example hospice and palliative treatment, they should not just be offered euthanasia as the only possibility. Far more research and funding needs to be given to developing hospice and palliative care. It is mostly the case, if people are informed of the other possibilities, they are then far less likely, to choose the option of euthanasia.

6. Difficulties of euthanasia

The subject of euthanasia stands at the cross-roads of many areas of conflict, for instance, between the laws of the state and the right to individual determination, between the medical ethics of providing treatment and withholding treatment, between the morality of saving life and taking life etc. In addition, it is very difficult to differentiate between the different forms of euthanasia within any individual case, and also, to determine, what may be punishable by law or not. Moreover, the issue of euthanasia is always being redefined, both, politically and ethically, and needs to be discussed over and over again. Particularly important questions, relating to the euthanasia-debate are:

→ Who, with certainty, can define, that a patient is „incurably ill" and has no hope of recovery?
→ Who would control the misuse of euthanasia?
→ Who would make sure, that the patient is not kept alive against his will?
→ Who could ensure, that the wishes of the patient are carried out, when the patient can no longer articulate his own needs?
→ Who has the right, to tell a terminally ill person, in unbearable pain, that they must continue to suffer?
→ Who would take responsibility for the decision, to carry out euthanasia?
→ Who should be the one to carry out active euthanasia?
→ Until what stage of the process is the patient fully able to decide?
→ Who is able to decide, if the patient's wish is a genuine wish to die or only a temporary psychological depression?
→ Is euthanasia compatible with human dignity? Or vice versa: Is keeping a person alive against his will compatible with human dignity? What is a dignified life? What is a dignified death?
→ etc. …the range of questions is endless...

7. Arguments in favour of and against euthanasia

As well as the legal approach to solving the difficulties of euthanasia, people try to find the answers to the previously mentioned questions within a mainly ethical-philosophical framework. Doctors especially, have to deal with these questions over and over again, because the answers will be, in the end, the basis of their decisions. With technical progress in general, and particularly in the fields of medicine and natural-science, it has become possible to influence both the creation and the demise of human beings. But people have to take responsibility for the use or none-use of these possibilities. Such a responsibility can be a lot for an individual and this person is only able, to do justice to this responsibility, if he faces up to all the complex issues involved. People's opinions are largely based on their own particular moral belief system. These opinions range from the belief, that every human being has the right to live, but also the right to die, to the belief, that people, under no circumstances have the right, to determine the ending of human life. The last position is particularly influenced by the use of euthanasia by the Nazis, where they determined, what particular groups of people had the right to continue living. Those, who are in favour of euthanasia, see euthanasia as a possibility, to end a person's life in dignity. They believe, that every patient, who no longer has the physical capability to commit suicide, should be provided with the possibility, to let himself die. Those who object to euthanasia, believe, that a wish to die shows only a lack of adequate societal support and good councelling. They ask for an improvement in pain-relief therapy and the quality of hospice-care, instead of the legalization of euthanasia. They claim, that legalization would open the floodgates to misuse and that it would invite the danger, that the taking of life would find general social acceptance.

Some examples of the pro- and contra-arguments:

Arguments in favour of euthanasia	Arguments against euthanasia
Every human being has the right to live but also the right to die.	People, under no circumstances, have the authorization to decide about the ending of a life.
Euthanasia holds the possibility to end a person's life in dignity.	The wish to die shows only lack of adequate societal support and good counselling. An improvement of pain-relief therapy and hospice-care at the end of a patient's life is what is needed instead of the legalization of euthanasia.

Every patient, who has lost the ability to commit suicide, for instance, because of weakened physical health, should be provided with the possibility to let himself die.	Legalization would open the floodgates to misuse.
Death is a right of everybody. (This is even implied legally where a person who attempts suicide is not punishable by law.)	Legalization would invite the danger that the taking of life would find general social acceptance.
There is no the danger of a repetition of genocide as happened in history, if a concrete regulation is given to doctors, in which euthanasia is strictly controlled.	If doctors are given the right to decide about a patient and his life at their own discretion, this is only one step away from mass-euthanasia as happened in German history.
	Elderly people could feel under pressure to seek euthanasia, because they don't want to put a financial strain on society or their families any longer.

Both, advocates and opponents of euthanasia, share the opinion, that there is great lack of clarity on this issue, due to the uncertainty of the laws, regarding euthanasia, and the legal gray area, in which cases of euthanasia can only be judged by the existing laws of murder, manslaughter etc. That's, why a concrete legal regulation is long overdue.

The most recent polls about euthanasia (from polling-firms like Forsa and Emnid) showed, that from the group of people questioned, who had not been informed beforehand about alternatives, 74 % were in favour of euthanasia, 20 % were against, and 6 % abstained. From the people surveyed, who had informed about alternatives like palliative medicine or hospice, 35 % were in favour of euthanasia and 55 % were against it.

8. Conclusion

It is my view that there can be no hard and fast moral or ethical positions on euthanasia. Every individual case brings up the same questions and problems, which I've tried to touch on in this presentation. One can find reasonable arguments for and against its use, but in the end, this topic is so complex, that general all-purpose answers to the questions posed, do not do it justice. A continued and, if possible, not too emotional examination of the questions is necessary, because we can only find possible solutions in an ongoing discussion. A solution is needed, that allows enough flexibility, and security for the people affected, both, the patients and medical practitioners.

9. Literatur

Benzenhöfer, Udo (1999): *Der gute Tod?* München: Beck.

Hohenstein, Anne (2003): *Die Einführung der aktiven Sterbehilfe in der Bundesrepublik Deutschland: Lässt sich das Recht auf den eigenen Tod verfassungsrechtlich begründen?* Berlin: Logos.

Schockenhoff, Eberhard (1991): *Sterbehilfe und Menschenwürde*, Regensburg: Pustet.

Schumpelick, Volker (2003): *Klinische Sterbehilfe und Menschenwürde. Ein deutsch-niederländischer Dialog.* Freiburg: Herder.

www.dieterwunderlich.de/sterbehilfe.htm

www.dignitas.ch

www.thieme.de/viamedici/medizin/aerztliches_handeln/palliativmedizin_interview.html

home.tiscali.de/sterbehilfe/

www.uwenowak.de/arbeiten/sterbehilfe.xhtml

de.wikipedia.org/wiki/Sterbehilfe

Appendix: Well-known cases of euthanasia

There are cases which clearly show that incurably ill people sometimes feel their circumstances to be unbearable and ask for help to die, although they have loving support and full medical care. It is not only the physical pain that is agonizing to them, but the lack of human dignity they feel in their situation.

Two well-known cases of euthanasia, which revived the discussion about euthanasia in Germany:

Ramón Sampedro (1943 – 1998)

→ from Spain

→ paralyzed in a diving accident at the age of 26

→ fought for his right to an assisted suicide for the next 29 years

→ due to his paralysis, he was physically unable to commit suicide

→ he argued that suicide was a right and that he was being denied that right

→ he sought legal advice concerning his right to an assisted suicide

→ his case drew attention from across Spain and also a significant following worldwide

→ he died in January 1998, aged 55 from potassium cyanide poisoning

→ his close friend Ramona Maneiro admitted to providing him with a cyanide-laced drink and a straw

→ he was the subject of the 2004 Spanish movie, *Mar adentro*

Terri Schiavo (1963 – 2005)

→ A woman from Florida whose unusual medical and family circumstances and attendant legal battles fueled intense media attention and led to several high-profile court decisions and involvement by prominent politicians and interest groups.

→ Schiavo experienced cardiac arrest and collapsed in her home in early 1990, incurring massive brain damage.

→ She remained in a coma for ten weeks. Within three years, she was diagnosed to be in a coma vigile state with little chance of recovery.

→ Beginning in 1998, Schiavo's husband (and guardian) petitioned the courts to remove the gastric feeding tube keeping Schiavo alive.

→ Schiavo's parents fought a series of legal battles opposing her husband. The courts consistently found that Schiavo was in a coma vigile and had made credible statements that she would not want to be kept alive on a machine.

→ By March 2005, the legal history around the Schiavo case included fourteen appeals and innumerable motions, petitions, and hearings in the Florida courts; five suits in Federal District Court; Florida legislation struck down by the Supreme Court of Florida; a subpoena by a congressional committee in an attempt to qualify Schiavo for *witness protection*; federal legislation; and four denials of certiorari from the Supreme Court of the United States.

→ Despite these interventions, the courts continued to find that Schiavo was in a coma vigile with no hope for recovery, and would want to cease life support.

→ Her feeding tube was removed a third and final time on March 18, 2005.

→ She died at a hospice on March 31, 2005, at the age of 41.